Congratulations to:

_____

Guests

_____

_____

_____

_____

_____

_____

_____

_____

_____

_____

Thoughts and Memories

_____

_____

_____

_____

_____

_____

_____

_____

_____

_____

Guests

_____

_____

_____

_____

_____

_____

_____

_____

_____

_____

_____

Thoughts and Memories

_____

_____

_____

_____

_____

_____

_____

_____

_____

_____

_____

Guests

Thoughts and Memories

Guests

_____

_____

_____

_____

_____

_____

_____

_____

_____

_____

_____

Thoughts and Memories

_____

_____

_____

_____

_____

_____

_____

_____

_____

_____

_____

Guests

_____

_____

_____

_____

_____

_____

_____

_____

_____

_____

_____

Thoughts and Memories

_____

_____

_____

_____

_____

_____

_____

_____

_____

_____

_____

Guests

_____

_____

_____

_____

_____

_____

_____

_____

_____

_____

_____

Thoughts and Memories

_____

_____

_____

_____

_____

_____

_____

_____

_____

_____

_____

Guests

Thoughts and Memories

_____

_____

_____

_____

_____

_____

_____

_____

_____

_____

Guests

Thoughts and Memories

_____

_____

_____

_____

_____

_____

_____

_____

_____

_____

Guests

_____

_____

_____

_____

_____

_____

_____

_____

_____

_____

_____

Thoughts and Memories

_____

_____

_____

_____

_____

_____

_____

_____

_____

_____

_____

Guests

_____

_____

_____

_____

_____

_____

_____

_____

_____

_____

Thoughts and Memories

_____

_____

_____

_____

_____

_____

_____

_____

_____

_____

Guests

Thoughts and Memories

_____

_____

_____

_____

_____

_____

_____

_____

_____

_____

_____

Guests

Thoughts and Memories

Guests

_____

_____

_____

_____

_____

_____

_____

_____

_____

_____

Thoughts and Memories

_____

_____

_____

_____

_____

_____

_____

_____

_____

_____

Guests

_____

_____

_____

_____

_____

_____

_____

_____

_____

_____

_____

Thoughts and Memories

_____

_____

_____

_____

_____

_____

_____

_____

_____

_____

_____

Guests

Thoughts and Memories

_____

_____

_____

_____

_____

_____

_____

_____

_____

_____

Guests

_____

_____

_____

_____

_____

_____

_____

_____

_____

_____

Thoughts and Memories

_____

_____

_____

_____

_____

_____

_____

_____

_____

_____

Guests

Thoughts and Memories

_____

_____

_____

_____

_____

_____

_____

_____

_____

_____

Guests

_____

_____

_____

_____

_____

_____

_____

_____

_____

_____

Thoughts and Memories

_____

_____

_____

_____

_____

_____

_____

_____

_____

_____

Guests

_____

_____

_____

_____

_____

_____

_____

_____

_____

_____

Thoughts and Memories

_____

_____

_____

_____

_____

_____

_____

_____

_____

_____

Guests

_____

_____

_____

_____

_____

_____

_____

_____

_____

_____

_____

Thoughts and Memories

_____

_____

_____

_____

_____

_____

_____

_____

_____

_____

_____

Guests

Thoughts and Memories

_____   _____

_____   _____

_____   _____

_____   _____

_____   _____

_____   _____

_____   _____

_____   _____

_____   _____

_____   _____

Guests

Thoughts and Memories

Guests

_____

_____

_____

_____

_____

_____

_____

_____

_____

_____

_____

Thoughts and Memories

_____

_____

_____

_____

_____

_____

_____

_____

_____

_____

_____

Guests

_____

_____

_____

_____

_____

_____

_____

_____

_____

_____

Thoughts and Memories

_____

_____

_____

_____

_____

_____

_____

_____

_____

_____

Guests

Thoughts and Memories

_____ _____

_____ _____

_____ _____

_____ _____

_____ _____

_____ _____

_____ _____

_____ _____

_____ _____

_____ _____

_____ _____

Guests

_____

_____

_____

_____

_____

_____

_____

_____

_____

_____

_____

Thoughts and Memories

_____

_____

_____

_____

_____

_____

_____

_____

_____

_____

_____

Guests

_____

_____

_____

_____

_____

_____

_____

_____

_____

_____

Thoughts and Memories

_____

_____

_____

_____

_____

_____

_____

_____

_____

_____

Guests

_____

_____

_____

_____

_____

_____

_____

_____

_____

_____

_____

Thoughts and Memories

_____

_____

_____

_____

_____

_____

_____

_____

_____

_____

_____

Guests

Thoughts and Memories

Guests

Thoughts and Memories

_____

_____

_____

_____

_____

_____

_____

_____

_____

_____

_____

_____

_____

_____

_____

_____

_____

_____

_____

_____

Guests

Thoughts and Memories

_____

_____

_____

_____

_____

_____

_____

_____

_____

_____

_____

Guests

Thoughts and Memories

Guests

_____

_____

_____

_____

_____

_____

_____

_____

_____

_____

Thoughts and Memories

_____

_____

_____

_____

_____

_____

_____

_____

_____

_____

Guests

Thoughts and Memories

Guests

_____

_____

_____

_____

_____

_____

_____

_____

_____

_____

_____

Thoughts and Memories

_____

_____

_____

_____

_____

_____

_____

_____

_____

_____

_____

Guests

Thoughts and Memories

Guests

_____

_____

_____

_____

_____

_____

_____

_____

_____

_____

Thoughts and Memories

_____

_____

_____

_____

_____

_____

_____

_____

_____

_____

Guests

_____

_____

_____

_____

_____

_____

_____

_____

_____

_____

Thoughts and Memories

_____

_____

_____

_____

_____

_____

_____

_____

_____

_____

Guests

_____

_____

_____

_____

_____

_____

_____

_____

_____

_____

Thoughts and Memories

_____

_____

_____

_____

_____

_____

_____

_____

_____

_____

Guests

_____

_____

_____

_____

_____

_____

_____

_____

_____

_____

Thoughts and Memories

_____

_____

_____

_____

_____

_____

_____

_____

_____

_____

Guests

_____

_____

_____

_____

_____

_____

_____

_____

_____

_____

Thoughts and Memories

_____

_____

_____

_____

_____

_____

_____

_____

_____

_____

Guests

Thoughts and Memories

Guests

_____

_____

_____

_____

_____

_____

_____

_____

_____

_____

_____

Thoughts and Memories

_____

_____

_____

_____

_____

_____

_____

_____

_____

_____

_____

Guests

_____

_____

_____

_____

_____

_____

_____

_____

_____

_____

_____

Thoughts and Memories

_____

_____

_____

_____

_____

_____

_____

_____

_____

_____

_____

Guests

Thoughts and Memories

Guests

Thoughts and Memories

Guests

_____

_____

_____

_____

_____

_____

_____

_____

_____

_____

_____

Thoughts and Memories

_____

_____

_____

_____

_____

_____

_____

_____

_____

_____

_____

Guests

_____

_____

_____

_____

_____

_____

_____

_____

_____

_____

Thoughts and Memories

_____

_____

_____

_____

_____

_____

_____

_____

_____

_____

Guests

Thoughts and Memories

Guests

_____

_____

_____

_____

_____

_____

_____

_____

_____

_____

_____

Thoughts and Memories

_____

_____

_____

_____

_____

_____

_____

_____

_____

_____

_____

Guests

_____

_____

_____

_____

_____

_____

_____

_____

_____

_____

_____

Thoughts and Memories

_____

_____

_____

_____

_____

_____

_____

_____

_____

_____

_____

Guests

_____

_____

_____

_____

_____

_____

_____

_____

_____

_____

Thoughts and Memories

_____

_____

_____

_____

_____

_____

_____

_____

_____

_____

Guests

_____

_____

_____

_____

_____

_____

_____

_____

_____

_____

Thoughts and Memories

_____

_____

_____

_____

_____

_____

_____

_____

_____

_____

Guests

_____

_____

_____

_____

_____

_____

_____

_____

_____

_____

Thoughts and Memories

_____

_____

_____

_____

_____

_____

_____

_____

_____

_____

Guests

Thoughts and Memories

_____

_____

_____

_____

_____

_____

_____

_____

_____

_____

Guests

Thoughts and Memories

_____

_____

_____

_____

_____

_____

_____

_____

_____

_____

_____

_____

_____

_____

_____

_____

Guests

_____

_____

_____

_____

_____

_____

_____

_____

_____

_____

Thoughts and Memories

_____

_____

_____

_____

_____

_____

_____

_____

_____

_____

Guests

Thoughts and Memories

_____

_____

_____

_____

_____

_____

_____

_____

_____

_____

_____

_____

_____

_____

_____

_____

_____

_____

Guests

Thoughts and Memories

_____

_____

_____

_____

_____

_____

_____

_____

_____

Guests

Thoughts and Memories

_____

_____

_____

_____

_____

_____

_____

_____

_____

_____

Guests

Thoughts and Memories

_____

_____

_____

_____

_____

_____

_____

_____

_____

_____

Guests	Thoughts and Memories
_____	_____
_____	_____
_____	_____
_____	_____
_____	_____
_____	_____
_____	_____
_____	_____
_____	_____
_____	_____

Guests

_____

_____

_____

_____

_____

_____

_____

_____

_____

_____

Thoughts and Memories

_____

_____

_____

_____

_____

_____

_____

_____

_____

_____

Guests

Thoughts and Memories

_____

_____

_____

_____

_____

_____

_____

_____

_____

_____

_____

_____

_____

_____

_____

_____

_____

_____

_____

_____

Guests

_____

_____

_____

_____

_____

_____

_____

_____

_____

_____

Thoughts and Memories

_____

_____

_____

_____

_____

_____

_____

_____

_____

_____

Guests

Thoughts and Memories

Guests

_____

_____

_____

_____

_____

_____

_____

_____

_____

_____

Thoughts and Memories

_____

_____

_____

_____

_____

_____

_____

_____

_____

_____

Guests

Thoughts and Memories

Guests

Thoughts and Memories

Guests

Thoughts and Memories

Guests

Thoughts and Memories

Guests

_____

_____

_____

_____

_____

_____

_____

_____

_____

Thoughts and Memories

_____

_____

_____

_____

_____

_____

_____

_____

_____

Guests

                # Thoughts and Memories

_____

_____

_____

_____

_____

_____

_____

_____

_____

_____

Guests

_____

_____

_____

_____

_____

_____

_____

_____

_____

_____

Thoughts and Memories

_____

_____

_____

_____

_____

_____

_____

_____

_____

_____

Guests

_____

_____

_____

_____

_____

_____

_____

_____

_____

Thoughts and Memories

_____

_____

_____

_____

_____

_____

_____

_____

_____

Guests

Thoughts and Memories

_____

_____

_____

_____

_____

_____

_____

_____

_____

_____

Guests

_____

_____

_____

_____

_____

_____

_____

_____

_____

_____

Thoughts and Memories

_____

_____

_____

_____

_____

_____

_____

_____

_____

_____

Guests

Thoughts and Memories

_____

_____

_____

_____

_____

_____

_____

_____

_____

_____

_____

_____

_____

_____

_____

_____

_____

_____

Guests

_____

_____

_____

_____

_____

_____

_____

_____

_____

_____

Thoughts and Memories

_____

_____

_____

_____

_____

_____

_____

_____

_____

_____

Guests

_____

_____

_____

_____

_____

_____

_____

_____

_____

Thoughts and Memories

_____

_____

_____

_____

_____

_____

_____

_____

_____

Guests

_____

_____

_____

_____

_____

_____

_____

_____

_____

_____

Thoughts and Memories

_____

_____

_____

_____

_____

_____

_____

_____

_____

_____

Guests

_____

_____

_____

_____

_____

_____

_____

_____

_____

Thoughts and Memories

_____

_____

_____

_____

_____

_____

_____

_____

_____

Guests

_____

_____

_____

_____

_____

_____

_____

_____

_____

_____

Thoughts and Memories

_____

_____

_____

_____

_____

_____

_____

_____

_____

_____

Guests

Thoughts and Memories

_____

_____

_____

_____

_____

_____

_____

_____

_____

_____

_____

_____

_____

_____

_____

_____

_____

_____

_____

_____

Guests

_____

_____

_____

_____

_____

_____

_____

_____

_____

_____

Thoughts and Memories

_____

_____

_____

_____

_____

_____

_____

_____

_____

_____

Guests

_____

_____

_____

_____

_____

_____

_____

_____

_____

_____

Thoughts and Memories

_____

_____

_____

_____

_____

_____

_____

_____

_____

_____

Guests

_____

_____

_____

_____

_____

_____

_____

_____

_____

Thoughts and Memories

_____

_____

_____

_____

_____

_____

_____

_____

_____

Guests

_____

_____

_____

_____

_____

_____

_____

_____

_____

_____

Thoughts and Memories

_____

_____

_____

_____

_____

_____

_____

_____

_____

_____

Guests

Thoughts and Memories

_____

_____

_____

_____

_____

_____

_____

_____

_____

_____

Guests

Thoughts and Memories

_____

_____

_____

_____

_____

_____

_____

_____

_____

_____

Guests

_____

_____

_____

_____

_____

_____

_____

_____

_____

Thoughts and Memories

_____

_____

_____

_____

_____

_____

_____

_____

_____

Guests

Thoughts and Memories

_____

_____

_____

_____

_____

_____

_____

_____

_____

Guests

Thoughts and Memories

_____

_____

_____

_____

_____

_____

_____

_____

_____

_____

_____

_____

_____

_____

_____

_____

_____

_____

_____

_____

Guests

_____

_____

_____

_____

_____

_____

_____

_____

_____

_____

Thoughts and Memories

_____

_____

_____

_____

_____

_____

_____

_____

_____

_____

Guests

Thoughts and Memories

_____

_____

_____

_____

_____

_____

_____

_____

_____

_____

_____

Guests

Thoughts and Memories

Guests

_____

_____

_____

_____

_____

_____

_____

_____

_____

_____

Thoughts and Memories

_____

_____

_____

_____

_____

_____

_____

_____

_____

_____

Guests

_____

_____

_____

_____

_____

_____

_____

_____

_____

_____

Thoughts and Memories

_____

_____

_____

_____

_____

_____

_____

_____

_____

_____

Guests

_____

_____

_____

_____

_____

_____

_____

_____

_____

_____

Thoughts and Memories

_____

_____

_____

_____

_____

_____

_____

_____

_____

_____

Guests

Thoughts and Memories

_____

_____

_____

_____

_____

_____

_____

_____

_____

_____

_____

_____

_____

_____

_____

_____

_____

_____

Guests

_____

_____

_____

_____

_____

_____

_____

_____

_____

_____

Thoughts and Memories

_____

_____

_____

_____

_____

_____

_____

_____

_____

_____

Guests

Thoughts and Memories

_____

_____

_____

_____

_____

_____

_____

_____

_____

Guests

_____

_____

_____

_____

_____

_____

_____

_____

_____

_____

Thoughts and Memories

_____

_____

_____

_____

_____

_____

_____

_____

_____

_____

Guests

Thoughts and Memories

_____

_____

_____

_____

_____

_____

_____

_____

_____

_____

_____

_____

_____

_____

_____

_____

_____

_____

_____

_____

Guests

_____

_____

_____

_____

_____

_____

_____

_____

_____

Thoughts and Memories

_____

_____

_____

_____

_____

_____

_____

_____

_____

Guests

Thoughts and Memories

Printed in Great Britain
by Amazon